A Thorn Between the Roses: Esther, Jonah, and Ruth

Jo Ann Sherbine

authorHOUSE®

AuthorHouse™
1663 Liberty Drive
Bloomington, IN 47403
www.authorhouse.com
Phone: 1-800-839-8640

Published by AuthorHouse 1/9/2013

ISBN: 978-1-4817-0090-0 (sc)
ISBN: 978-1-4817-0089-4 (e)

Dedication

This volume is dedicated to all those with whom I have been privileged to participate in Bible study. The individuals are too numerous to mention, but include members of our Neighborhood Bible Study Group in Bennettsville, SC; Circles in First Baptist Church of Cheraw, SC, Thomas Memorial Baptist Church of Bennettsville, and First Baptist Church at the Mall in Lakeland, FL; the Ruth Sunday School Class at Thomas Memorial; members of the St. Paul's Episcopal Church Wednesday Bible Study in Bennettsville; and the Highland Fairways Wednesday Morning Bible Study Group in Lakeland. Each listener and each leader in these groups has been an encouragement and an inspiration, and has contributed to the promise Jesus made to us of giving us not only life, but life abundantly.

Introduction

This book reintroduces three well-known persons from the Old Testament. The narratives with which we are familiar tell their stories. In each story there are elements that raise some serious theological questions, not the least of which is why they were included in the canon of Scripture in the first place. This book does not pretend to answer any of those questions, or even to address them. It is simply a retelling of the stories in rhyme, at some points very rough rhyme.

Sometimes, for some people, rhymed lines are easier to remember, or memorize, than straight prose. If that works for you, the reader, then so much the better. I have tried to use language that does not require you to have a dictionary at your elbow, or a grammar reference to decode. Occasionally you may encounter a word that by itself you would not recognize, but within the context of the story its meaning will be clear; it was probably selected for its "rhyme factor" and not to deliberately challenge your reading.

Esther has always been one of my favorite Bible "characters". She did not begin her royal life with any particular courage or boldness. But when put in a position of having to choose risk for the good of her people over personal safety and security, she discovered courage she didn't know she had. Given the eventual result of her choice, plus the wise plans she devised, we can see the hand of God at work in her life. His Name, however, is never mentioned in the account of Esther's life as the wife of a pagan king.

Jonah, on the other hand, encountered the voice of God early in his story — and chose to pretend he had not heard anything. The God of second chances, however, arranged for his rescue from the big fish, accepted his repentance, allowed him to preach in Nineveh, and even tried to reason with him in his resentment of the Ninevites' eager acceptance of the message of redemption. The dialogue between Jonah and God provides the impetus for Jonah's story.

Ruth, as a Moabitess, knew of God only through the life and witness of her mother-in-law. Born and reared in a land of one of Israel's enemies, she was nevertheless eager to return with Naomi to Naomi's homeland, where God was worshiped. Ruth was discipled by Naomi, as well as by Boaz as he demonstrated kindness and sensitivity to her needs.

These three — Esther, Jonah, and Ruth — teach us that God will meet us wherever we are and lead us as far as we are willing to be led. The Feast of Purim, still celebrated by Jews around the world, is directly attributable to Esther's decisions and actions. Jesus Christ, Savior of the world, was, in His humanity, a direct descendant of Ruth. Sadly, we are left wondering about Jonah: he was still pouting at the end of his book, and we simply don't know if he ever rejoiced in the salvation of so many of the Ninevites and God's decision to not destroy the city.

Please read the book with your Bible on your lap. Read the Scripture before you read the corresponding chapter in the book. Ponder as you read, considering what your responses and reactions might have been in similar circumstances. Read prayerfully and thoughtfully, seeking a word from the Lord for your own life. He is still in charge of the circumstances of our lives.

Esther 1

From India to Ethiopia
Xerxes was the king.
Over one hundred-twenty-seven provinces
His authority the heralds would bring.

Shushan was the center
Of the empire deep and broad;
Feasts and popularity
Left little room for God.

Third year on the throne –
It was time to show his wealth
Before the Medes and Persians
And all who drank to his health.

Six months of celebrations
And still he wasn't done;
Now to entertain the palace
With revelry and fun.

The garden court was awesome
With its hangings, silver, and gold,
Four-colored pavements of marble
And drinking vessels of old.

No one was forced to drink:
That was the king's command.
However, it was obvious
That many had tipped a hand.

Entertaining the women of court
Queen Vashti did her part,
With food and fun and fellowship;
None had a lonely heart.

By the end of the week for the palace,
Full of mirth, and wine and gall,
The king was ready for one last show —
To share Vashti's beauty with all.

He sent the servants to fetch her,
But she refused to come,
Knowing he wanted only a spectacle
Of her body before the throng.

Of course the king was angry,
And called on seven princes for advice;
They all knew that whatever happened
Was not going to be nice.

According to Memucan,
Spokesman for the others,
The greatest crime of Vashti had been
An "attack" upon the brothers.

If the queen could defy the king,
No man in the kingdom was safe
From a wife who would take control
And try to keep her man "in his place".

Memucan's plan, then, was designed
To send a message strong:
Any wife who refused her husband's desires
Would be punished severely for the wrong.

Vashti would be the example:
Banished and deprived of her role,
Replaced by someone better than she
Who would not torment the king's soul.

The punishment was so severe —
Or so Memucan surmised —

That wives all over the kingdom
Would become their husband's "prize".

The king was so happy with this advice
He lost no time in adhering
By sending letters throughout the kingdom
Ordering husbands to be more commandeering.

Did chauvinism start right here
With this king and queen?
Who knows; but greater disrespect
Rarely has been seen.

Esther 2

The king recovered from his anger
And remembered Vashti the queen,
Who had been banished from his presence,
Nevermore in the court to be seen.

Advisors gave him counsel
For replacing the beautiful queen:
Invite all the fair young virgins
To come to the palace and preen.

The king would have many choices
From whom to select his new queen.
She would have counsel and guidance
Because she no doubt would be "green".

Mordecai was working in the palace,
A Jewish captive in the land;
He was foster-father to Esther,
Who resided with him in Shushan.

Esther was brought to the palace with others,
But singled out for special care:
Given seven personal maidens
And the best rooms in the lair.

Esther had a secret.
Advised by Mordecai,
The fact of her Jewish heritage
Was not heralded on high.

Mordecai kept an eye on her
Every day for one whole year,
Until it was Esther's turn
To visit the king without fear.

She had been carefully primped and trained
For this climactic night:
She would go before the king
For her chance to earn his delight.

That one solitary night
Would be all she'd have with the king,
Unless he requested her by name
To return — and make his heart sing.

Now Esther was pure and pretty:
She needed no make-up and stuff
To show what she had to offer;
She was natural, with no fluff.

It only took the one visit
For Xerses to make up his mind:
The queen's crown went straight to Esther;
He recognized her as one of a kind.

The king sent out announcements
And planned an introductory feast;
He was anxious to show off her beauty —
And the "inner" was not the least.

Esther clung tightly to her secret,
And Mordecai hovered nearby,
Encouraging her to be faithful
While not really living a lie.

Mordecai caught wind of a plot
Against the life of the king;
He passed the info on to Esther,
Knowing she would do the right thing.

She reported the plot to Xerses,
Along with Mordecai's name;

An investigation ensued
And revealed the conspirators' game.

The evil men were punished
By hanging from a tree.
Mordecai's loyalty was recorded
In chronicles Xerses could read.

Esther 3

Things were rather peaceful now
For the kingdom and its king;
Conspirators had been hanged –
The last troublesome thing.

The king promoted Haman
To second in command;
All the princes and servants
Were to bow and kiss his hand.

Almost everyone complied;
Only Mordecai refused to bow.
We do not know exactly why,
But by Haman he was not cowed.

Questioned by the servants
Who hung around Shushan's gate,
Mordecai refused to answer,
Apparently sealing his fate.

Chance after chance they gave him,
But his silence wore them out;
So they reported to Haman
This man who king's orders did flout.

One thing they knew about Mordecai:
He had told them he was a Jew.
They reported this too to Haman,
Not knowing what he would do.

Mordecai's refusal to bow,
And then his Jewishness, too,
Surfaced all of Haman's wrath
And no doubt turned his language blue.

The plan he concocted was large:
To punish all the Jews in the land
Rather than only Mordecai;
Haman would not let one Jew stand.

It took Haman one full year,
From April to the following March,
To get his evil plan aligned
With actions the king would not parch.

So Haman went before the king
With words flattering, and only half-true,
About the unique lifestyle of "this group" -
And he proposed what the king should do.

Haman suggested total destruction
Without mentioning the Jews by name;
He offered over nineteen million dollars
For the winning of his little game.

Whether the king was lured by the money,
Or angered by defiance of his law,
He gave his signet ring to Haman
With authority to wipe out the flaws.

Haman was given full power
And the money to support his plan.
We can only envision the glint in his eye
As he considered getting his man.

Haman called in all the scribes
And dictated his orders with glee:
All Jews throughout the kingdom
Would be slaughtered with no mercy

The scribes wrote in all the dialects,
And the orders were sent far and wide;

Governors and rulers in every province
Knew that no Jew was to abide.

Even the day was established
For the mass annihilation:
The thirteenth day of the following March
Would eliminate God's nation.

Men and women, old and young —
Every Jew was doomed to perish;
The spoils from this victory
Would become Haman's to cherish.

All the provincial leaders
Were given almost a year
To get ready to carry out orders
That would elicit many a tear.

Once the decree had gone forth,
The king and Haman breathed deep;
They finally sat down to celebrate,
Before a sound night's sleep.

But around the city of Shushan,
Close by where the palace sat,
People were perplexed and troubled;
No doubt somebody smelled a rat.

Esther 4

Grieved by Haman's orders,
Mordecai loudly cried;
Clothed in ashy sackcloth
He chose to live outside.

All throughout the kingdom
Reactions were the same:
Jews – God's chosen people –
Foresaw the end of their name.

Weeping, wailing, fasting -
Their grief had them lying prone.
Great mourning overtook them;
They felt abandoned and alone.

Esther heard of their reactions,
And of Mordecai's grieving, too;
At first she knew not the reason,
So she sought for something to do.

She sent clean, fresh clothes to Mordecai;
He refused her charitable gift.
So she sought an explanation,
And Hatach breached the rift.

He went into the street of the city
And found Mordecai outside the king's gate.
Mordecai told him the story
Of Haman's devious hate.

Mordecai included the sum of money
In the report to Esther he sent,
That would be paid to the royal coffers
When every Jew had been spent.

Mordecai even sent a copy
Of the decree from Haman's hand
So Esther would have evidence
For the next step he had planned.

Mordecai sent word to Esther
That she should go before the king,
Explain her own ethnicity
And plead for her people's saving.

Hatach reported back to Esther
All that he had been told;
She sent him back to Mordecai
To remind him she couldn't be bold.

It seems that in the law books
Adhered to by the court,
No one could go before the king
Without an invitation of a particular sort:

Unless the king held out his scepter
To receive the suppliant one,
The visitor could be killed on the spot
And never see another sun.

For thirty days before this,
Esther had not been called to see the king.
She was understandably fearful
And preferred to her life to cling.

Mordecai, perhaps with a touch of anger,
Responded to Esther's fears:
She would not escape the execution
That had been decreed for her Jewish peers.

Mordecai saw her in her position
For just such a time as this,

And if she shirked her duty
Her entire family would be dismissed.

Esther did not procrastinate
In sending a message back to him:
"Gather the Jews in Shushan
And prepare for a large pray-in."

She commanded three days of fasting and praying,
Which she and her maids would do likewise;
And, bolstered by the support of her people,
She would go in and meet the king's eyes.

She no longer feared breaking the law
As much as letting her people down.
Her resolve: "If I perish, I perish,"
Was carried through the town.

Mordecai went out and rallied the Jews
For three days to fast and pray;
He himself was the example
To put the sackcloth away.

Developing a plan of action
Pulls us out of the sorrowful mood;
Having a goal and a purpose
Does not allow for time to brood.

Esther 5

When the three days of fasting and prayer
Had occurred among the Jews,
Esther dressed up in her finest,
In royalty's magnificent hues.

She stood in the inner court,
Within the king's line of sight,
Not knowing if he would receive her,
Or if this would be her last night.

He looked up, he saw her, he motioned,
Holding to her the scepter in his hand,
Granting her royal permission
To come before him and stand.

He apparently knew from her demeanor
That she had something on her mind,
So he gently instructed her to tell him
What from him she hoped to find.

He was willing to give half his kingdom
To show Esther, if not love, his respect;
But what she requested of him
He certainly did not expect.

She had prepared for the king a banquet,
And asked him to bring Haman along;
The king, who loved food and parties,
Knew not there was anything wrong.

The king sent a message to Haman
Inviting him to come with great haste.
While the men were wining and dining,
Esther knew the obstacle she faced.

Again the king made his offer,
Up to half his kingdom to share;
Again Esther's response, well-scripted,
Caught him by surprise, but seemed fair.

Esther invited the king and Haman
To join her again the next night
For another sit-down banquet,
To both the king's and Haman's delight.

Haman left that first night happy:
He was obviously a friend of the king;
He ignored Mordecai's lack of honor,
His own praises to go home and sing.

Haman called in his friends and wife Zaresh
And described his new lifestyle in terms
Designed to impress and self-honor,
With no regard for low-life worms.

But one lowly worm ruined his pleasure —
Mordecai the Jew at the king's gate —
Haman's glory and promotions and advancements
Did not remove his hate.

Zaresh, eager to stroke him
Concocted an evil plan:
Build a seventy-five foot gallows
Designed for only one man.

With Haman's new identity
As King Xerses' very best friend,
It should be an easy matter
To hang Mordecai and watch his end.

Then he could attend Esther's banquet
With nothing troubling his mind,
So very soon that same evening
He ordered gallows — a very high kind.

Esther 6

While Haman was home making plans with his wife,
The king rolled and tossed in his bed.
He finally requested the records be brought,
And he was enlightened as he read.

Two former chamberlains, disloyal and angry,
Against the king had crafted a plot;
Mordecai knew and alerted Queen Esther,
So the treasonous servants were caught.

On this sleepless night the king asked a question:
How had Mordecai ever been honored?
Loyal and faithful and meek at the gate —
To thank him, no one had bothered.

Plans came together in the king's court,
Then Haman showed up for a favor.
The king ushered him in and gave him a second,
A large public honor to savor.

Haman forgot his gallows request
When he thought in the parade he'd be grand:
Dressed in royal apparel, with a crown on his head
And the king's signet ring on his hand.

When Haman had described the horse and parade
That he expected the king to bestow,
The king turned the tables and told him instead
To prepare Mordecai for the grand show.

Not in a position the king to ignore,
Or to blatantly disobey,
Haman grudgingly did for Mordecai
All that before the king he had laid.

When the parade was over Haman went home,
And Mordecai returned to the gate;
Haman was grieving his great loss of face
And to friends and his wife mourned his fate.

With some sort of insight his listeners said
That before Mordecai Haman would not prevail;
Even these pagans knew that Mordecai's Jews
Would ultimately never fail.

With no consolation from wife and friends,
Haman sulked and pouted in shame.
He even forgot the second feast scheduled
'Til the king's messengers called his name.

Haman sighed and followed them to the court,
With fears and apprehension and dread;
What if Queen Esther and the king found out
That he wanted Mordecai dead?

Esther 7

Esther knew the secret –
Men like and enjoy good food -
So banquet number two
Was to establish the king's mood.

Remember, this was Xerxes,
The connoisseur of wine,
Willing to do anything
When he was invited to dine.

"What can I do, Queen Esther,
To fill your life with joy?
What is your request?"
He knew Esther had a ploy.

"I'll give you half the kingdom,
Any desire of your heart."
Esther was prepared to share,
Including Haman's part.

Submissive and respectful,
Yet bold in her request,
She reminded him she was a Jew,
And had been chosen as his best.

She laid the law before him –
All Jews were scheduled to be slain –
Haman's goal was to destroy
Her people: that was plain.

Esther was diplomatic,
Willing to compromise;
She would have accepted bondage,
But not her people's demise.

Xerxes had deferred much power
To Haman, the evil man;
Xerxes, perhaps drunk again,
Seemed unaware of the plan.

"Who is he, and where is he,
The man with the evil heart?"
Esther wasted neither time nor words
In pointing out Haman's cunning part.

We're not told if Haman was surprised,
But we do know he was afraid;
We can only imagine his reaction
When his scheme before Xerxes was laid.

The king, frustrated and angry,
Stomped out of the banquet room;
He had many things to consider,
All of which ended in doom.

Haman now knew who had the power
Over his future, his very life,
So he tried to come on to Queen Esther,
Even though she was his king's wife.

The king returned to the palace
And found Haman on Esther's bed;
Understandably furious,
He was ready for Haman's head.

When one of the king's attendants
Told him of the gallows already prepared —
For Mordecai's wrongful hanging —
The king gave orders — and glared.

"Hang Haman on his gallows,
And do not waste any time!"

Haman's evil and corruption
Had no reason or rhyme.

Jealousy? Power? Position?
What was his ultimate goal?
Whatever he thought would fulfill him
Cost him his very soul.

The gallows constructed for Mordecai
Took Haman to his tragic due;
The king's wrath was pacified,
And Esther had saved the Jews.

Esther 8

Esther explained to the king the connection
Between Mordecai and herself, the queen,
After the king had given her Haman's house
And riches beyond what most had ever seen.

The king gave his retrieved ring to Mordecai,
And a position of honor and trust.
Esther turned over to Mordecai Haman's house,
Then bowed before the king in the dust.

This time she approached her husband with tears
Being shed for laws still on the books.
She begged him to preserve her people, the Jews,
The heritage she and Mordecai never forsook.

The king gave new orders to Mordecai
For a communiqué to go through his land.
All the empire from India to Ethiopia
In the king's name would receive a new command.

All the scribes from the kingdom were gathered
So not one language or dialect would be missed.
A date was established for all Jews to gather
In their cities, and raise the victory fist.

Not only did the king demand preservation,
But vengeance was in his orders, too;
Those who attacked and assaulted Esther's people,
On March thirteenth would get their due.

The Jews were ordered to claim the power
Of each province in which they abode,
To claim all their enemies' spoils and goods;
On camels, horses, and mules the messengers rode.

The city of Shushan was glad and rejoiced
When they received the updated news;
Mordecai appeared in his royal array;
Ultimately, the Jews never would lose.

Light and honor and gladness and joy
Came to all Jewish people that day,
Because Esther the queen — once an orphan girl —
Had found courage to have her say.

The Jewish population grew out of the fear
As pagans saw how joyous and glad
Queen Esther's chosen, protected people were;
Everyone knew good had won out over bad.

Esther 9

On the day that had been appointed
For the Jews to be destroyed,
The tables were turned on their enemies
Because Haman's plans were now void.

Across the provinces of the king
The Jews gathered together in power;
Their enemies, now frozen with fear,
Sought refuge as they cowered.

Rulers and governors and deputies
Were all eager to help the Jews,
Fearful now of Mordecai,
Who communicated all the king's views.

In Shushan, the palace community,
Five hundred were killed that day,
Including the ten sons of Haman:
The families of evil men pay.

One power the Jews had been given,
That they opted not to employ,
Was the power to pillage for spoils
Of the enemies they destroyed.

On the thirteenth day of Adar,
When the slaughter was nearly ended,
The king requested a tally
And anything more Queen Esther intended.

He knew what happened in Shushan,
But wondered about numbers far and wide;
His respect for his queen was evident –
He kept her always at his side.

Esther, who had developed courage,
Had an answer ready for the king:
She asked for an extension in Shushan
Before the Jews' victory bells could ring.

So on the fourteenth day of Adar,
In Shushan the Jews killed three hundred more;
They hung Haman's dead sons on the gallows,
But again took no spoils, as before.

In the provinces far beyond Shushan,
Seventy-five thousand were killed in one day.
The Jews stood up for their identity,
Yet they did not claim spoils or prey.

On the fourteenth day of Adar,
Except in the town of Shushan,
The Jews rested from the executions
Of those who had threatened their land.

They enjoyed a great day of feasting,
Celebrating their new-found worth;
The Shushanites fought an extra day,
Then joined the others in their mirth.

For the Jews who were now safe from destruction,
Those two feasting days were glad.
They did not revel in the annihilation,
But shared with others whatever they had.

Mordecai, in his role now as leader,
Instituted a new Jewish feast:
The two-day Feast of Purim would acknowledge
When torment from their enemies had ceased.

Purim gets its name from Pur – the lot –
Which Haman had cast against Jews

Before Esther revealed his devious plan,
And caused a rewriting of the news.

Those two special days are still honored,
Though the years have come and gone,
As a memorial to their salvation,
And to what Mordecai and Queen Esther had done.

Mordecai sent letters throughout the land,
With words of truth and peace,
To confirm that the joy of Purim
And its generosity would not cease.

Esther 10

It appears King Xerses did a turn-around
Under the influence of Esther his queen;
He discovered his former lifestyle
Had left a lot of life unseen.

His power was now directed
To the protection of those under his rule;
Not only to those in his circle,
But also to those who had no "pull".

He named Mordecai his right-hand man
To deal with the Jews in his command;
Not only was Mordecai's influence great,
But he was accepted throughout the land.

He sought safety and wealth for his people,
And peace for all their seed.
For one who sat in sackcloth and ashes,
This was a new focus, indeed.

Throughout the book of Esther,
God's name is never named;
But His guiding hand of compassion and love
Gave Esther and Mordecai fame.

Jonah 1

God had a job for Jonah,
And Nineveh was the place;
Thousands of people lived there,
Doing evil before God's face.

Jonah's commission was to preach there,
And warn of punishment to come;
But he deeply hated Gentiles,
Although he was Abraham's son.

So Jonah chose to flee to Tarshish,
A journey from Joppa by ship;
He paid the fare and embarked,
Thinking to give God the slip.

Comfortable on board the ship,
Jonah found a corner to nap,
Oblivious to the stormy waves
That around the ship did slap.

The sailors on board were scared to death —
Threw overboard extra weight —
And prayed to their gods and idols
That the mad tempest would abate.

Jonah was apparently the only one
Who slept through the storm that day.
The captain eventually woke him,
Eager for Jonah also to pray.

Praying, but not believing,
The sailors decided to cast lots;
They employed some ancient method:
Straws, or coins, or stones with little dots.

Although God is not into gambling,
He controlled the results of their cast;
For the lot they drew fell on Jonah,
So he was interviewed at last.

The others knew nothing about him -
He had paid fare and boarded the ship —
But now they plied him with questions:
"Who are you?" and "Why on this trip?"

Surprisingly, Jonah gave witness:
A Hebrew, and believer in God,
Creator of the universe
Including heaven and sea and sod.

The men now really panicked:
Their gods in power could not compare.
Plus Jonah had confessed to them
Why he was really there.

They figured Jonah would have the solution
For the violence of waves and sea;
But Jonah, now conscience-driven,
Knew by this ship he could not flee.

He knew God's hand was in the storm,
Tossing the ship to and fro;
And so he told the sailors
That overboard he must go.

Those strong rowers resisted him
As long as their arms held out;
But the wind and storm would not relent,
So their prayer went up in a shout.

They pleaded for forgiveness
For solving their problem that way;

They also acknowledged the hand of God
In events of that fateful day.

Much as they hated to do it —
They were of a life-loving sort —
They picked Jonah up and tossed him,
Either from stern or from port.

The sea's raging ceased immediately,
As soon as Jonah hit the waves;
Now they feared God in a different way,
And made vows their souls to save.

Sacrifices and promises
They offered to God in their plight;
Happy to have the storm over,
Yet still recovering from their fright.

When Jonah hit the water
A big fish was waiting there;
Swallowed him whole without gagging —
Jonah was now in God's — and the fish's — care.

Jonah 2

From the belly of the very big fish
Jonah now felt compelled to speak;
His prayer of repentance arose to God
From the deep depths, not from a peak.

Jonah cried out from present experience,
No doubt with fear and real remorse;
He was well aware that God heard him,
And had placed him on this course.

He remembered being cast overboard,
Into the billows and waves of the sea;
He knew that awful gasp of drowning:
"I've been cast away from Thee!"

In both body and soul he floundered,
Wrapped in weeds he could not undo,
Until he reached very bottom
And acknowledged he was being pursued.

God brought Jonah's life up from corruption,
And to God's temple directed his prayer;
When his soul had fainted within him,
God assured him He was right there.

One lesson Jonah admitted to learning
Was not to trust in vanities of life,
Depending on self and self's preferences
Results in mercyless-ness and strife.

From where Jonah was at this point in time,
He had nothing to give to his Lord;
He offered a sacrifice of thanksgiving —
Without knowing the Lord's final word.

Salvation available only from God
Jonah confessed to the Lord from the deep;
He promised – intended – to pay the vows
He would now be unable to keep.

Then a most unusual occurrence
Once again changed Jonah's foreboding:
God told that big fish to vomit,
And soon Jonah he was unloading.

We know Jonah was upchucked on dry land.
Many questions remain, with no answers:
Where was he? Who saw him? How was he?
And did the fish have residual ulcers?

Jonah 3

The God of second chances
Spoke to Jonah a second time:
"Go and preach to Nineveh;
Preach to them My words, not thine."

Jonah needed no second invitation;
He had learned his lesson well.
He obeyed and went straight to Nineveh,
God's message of repentance to tell.

Nineveh was a large city,
Maybe sixty miles from one gate across;
Jonah went about a third of the way in,
And warned of the coming loss.

Forty days was God's timeline
Before arranging an overthrow;
The harvest was ripe and ready;
Apparently seed had already been sown.

The people responded promptly,
With sackcloth and ashes and fast.
When the king got the word he joined them;
Concern about image was past.

As he grieved for the future of his city,
The king published and sent a decree,
Forbidding men to feed their animals:
Even beasts were to suffer and grieve.

He decreed that all the Ninevites,
Man and beast, young and old, grown and small,
Would cry to the God Almighty
And repent of evil, one and all.

He apparently knew evil and violence
Prevailed in the city he ruled:
"Cry to God, turn away from evil!"
Is what his subjects were told.

The king implied in the decree he sent out
That it might already be too late;
He acknowledged God's anger with evil,
And the destruction that might still be their fate.

But God, Infinite love and forgiveness,
Saw genuine repentance and turning from sin,
So He forgave and withdrew His plans
To do the city of Nineveh in.

Jonah 4

Perhaps not surprisingly
Jonah was not a happy man;
In fact, he was very angry
That God had changed His plan.

He began to use God's goodness
As his excuse for running away:
Knowing God would ultimately spare Nineveh,
No matter what Jonah might say.

In fact, he was so angry
He wanted to die right now.
But God spoke gently to him,
And gave him space to wrinkle his brow.

So Jonah went out east of the city
And in its shadow set up a tent,
To watch what would happen in Nineveh,
The city to which he'd been sent.

God, with His usual compassion,
Caused a gourd to grow up for shade
To protect Jonah from glaring sunlight,
And allow his anger to fade.

Although Jonah was glad for the gourd,
There's no evidence he ever said "thank you."
He assumed that because he'd finally obeyed,
The Lord was giving him his due.

By next morning, however, a worm
Had eaten the vine and the gourd;
Then God sent a powerful east wind,
And Jonah was mad at the Lord.

God had a hard time believing
Jonah could pout and grouse about so;
But Jonah just wanted to die,
In misery from head to toe.

Then the Lord tried to apply His lesson
To the root of Jonah's pain:
He was selfish and self-centered,
And did not want the Lord to reign.

The Lord explained to Jonah,
In words easy to understand,
That Nineveh, that great city,
Had one-hundred-twenty-thousand children in its hand.

Little children, infants and toddlers,
Who not yet knew left hand from right;
These all would have been extinguished
Based on Jonah's plan of blight.

The God of second chances
Treats His whole creation well.
Whether Jonah ever saw it God's way,
We will never be able to tell.

Ruth 1

Famine came to Bethlehem
When there were judges in the land.
Food was scarce, so Elimelech
Gathered up his little band.

His wife Naomi and two young sons
To Moab journeyed with him.
We don't know if God led them there,
Or if this was Elimelech's whim.

Elimelech eventually died
And left Naomi alone with her boys.
They each took a wife from the Moabites,
But produced no grand-baby joys.

Mahlon and Chilion both died, too,
Leaving the three women alone.
Naomi heard that the famine was over,
And she wanted to go home.

The end of the famine was credited
To a visit from the Lord,
Who gave bread back to the Israelites —
Even those who had ignored His word.

So Naomi and the girls left for Judah,
With Bethlehem as their ultimate goal.
Then Naomi stopped and shared with them
A message from her mind, not her soul.

"Return to your mother's house," she said,
To Orpah and Ruth in turn.
"You've dealt so kindly with me and my sons
That you the Lord will not spurn.

"The Lord grant that you find find peace and rest,
And a new, kind husband to love."
Naomi then wept, and kissed the girls,
And commended them to God above.

Neither was eager to leave her;
Both said they wanted to go
To Bethlehem with Naomi;
All of their spirits were low.

Naomi used reason and logic
To explain why they should go back home:
She was too old for another husband,
And would have no more sons of her own.

Here Naomi's argument grew bitter,
As she blamed the Lord for her sorrowful state:
His hand had gone out against her,
And her sadness He would not abate.

All three then wept together.
Orpah kissed Naomi, ready to leave.
But Ruth refused to leave her
And paid no attention to Naomi's plea.

Ruth said, "I will not leave you,
Or return to my mother's abode.
Wherever you go, I'll go with you,
And where you lodge will be my home.

"Your people will become my people,
And I want to believe in your God.
Wherever you die, I'll die and be buried,
After in your homeland I've trod."

Naomi ceased her arguments
When she realized Ruth meant what she said.

So the two went on together
'Til they arrived in Bethlehem.

It seemed the city came out to greet them:
Naomi had come back to live.
But, bitter, she asked to be called Mara,
Since the Lord had taken back what He did give.

Naomi's joy had been depleted
By the circumstances of her life;
She blamed God for her affliction
And her tragedies, which were rife.

Naomi and Ruth settled in,
Although we're not told exactly where.
It was time for the harvest of barley,
But Naomi seemed not to care.

Ruth 2

Naomi had kin in Bethlehem,
At least on her husband's side.
She did not appeal to his power or his wealth,
But chose humbly with Ruth to abide.

Ruth knew her place as daughter-in-law,
To provide for Naomi and herself;
So she asked Naomi's permission
To glean in the harvest for health.

She went outside the city
And found a field ripe with grain;
She fell in behind the reapers
To gather whatever she could claim.

Although she did not know it,
And if she had it would have mattered nil,
Ruth was gathering in the field of Boaz,
The near kinsman with a role to fill.

When Boaz came to his reapers,
They shared respect "between me and thee":
Invoking the presence and blessing of God
In faith evident for all to see.

Boaz questioned his chief servant
About the damsel reaping in the field;
The servant knew she had come with Naomi
From Moab; that's all he could yield.

She had asked permission to gather
What sheaves the reapers left behind.
Given permission, she had worked hard;
An easy life was not on her mind.

Boaz then approached Ruth in the field
With a statement that resembled a command:
"Do not glean in anyone else's fields;
Stay with my maidens on my land."

He promised she'd have no discomfort
From the young men who were reaping the grain;
They'd received orders not to touch her,
And the orders had been very plain.

In the fields of Boaz, Naomi's relative,
Ruth was made to feel quite at home;
Water was available, and at lunchtime
She would eat with the others, not alone.

Ruth acknowledged Boaz's kindness
By bowing low before him, on the ground,
And seeking an explanation
For the generosity she had found.

Boaz was honest and forthright;
He knew all about her story.
He knew she'd left parents and homeland
To be with Naomi, without any glory.

He also knew she had come to trust
In the God of Israel – his God, too;
And he prayed that Ruth would receive
A reward for what she would do.

Ruth asked only for Boaz's favor,
Grateful that he was so friendly and kind;
She had lunch with Boaz and the reapers,
Then went out more grain to find.

Meanwhile Boaz cautioned his reapers
To deliberately drop some sheaves,

Which would relieve some of Ruth's effort,
Yet not give her a life of ease.

When evening came she was finished
With gleaning for that one day;
Then she went to beat out the barley,
Which was her and Naomi's pay.

She beat out over a bushel,
Then home to Naomi she went.
Naomi took what she thought she needed,
And with the remainder Ruth was content.

In starting the conversation,
Naomi inquired where Ruth had gleaned;
Ruth explained about her meeting with Boaz;
She did not know what that would mean.

Then Naomi explained the connection,
That Boaz was near next-of-kin,
And that in being kind to Ruth and Naomi,
He was honoring the dead — for them a win.

Ruth reported to Naomi
That Boaz had told her to come back,
To finish the harvest in his fields,
So neither food or safety would she lack.

With Boaz's order to Ruth,
Naomi readily agreed:
Ruth would stay by Boaz's maidens,
And work only in his fields, indeed.

Ruth did not have to decide
Where to go to work each day:
She gleaned through barley and wheat times,
And each night with Naomi she stayed.

Ruth 3

When harvesting time was over
And Ruth had completed her work,
Naomi came for a conversation.
Although he really had no duty to shirk,

Fact was that Boaz was kinsman,
And responsibility came with that role.
Naomi had a plan hatched for Ruth
That would touch Boaz's very soul.

Naomi knew from some source that Boaz
Was at nighttime winnowing grain,
Which meant he was at the threshing floor,
Which helped with the plan she had made.

She told Ruth to get cleaned up and dressed,
But not to go out until late;
Until Boaz was done eating and drinking,
Outside in the dark Ruth would wait.

Ruth would quietly wait, and watch
To see where Boaz would finally lie down;
Then she'd go in, uncover his feet,
And curl up under her gown.

Whether Ruth had ever heard of this custom,
We have no way of finding out;
But we know she respected Naomi,
So this strategy she did not doubt.

She did as Naomi had outlined —
Followed her plan to a tee;
When Boaz was full of food and drink,
He lay by the corn, heart-merry.

On tiptoe and almost without breathing,
Ruth sneaked into the threshing floor;
She uncovered his feet and lay down —
And no doubt kept her eye on the door.

At midnight something roused Boaz,
And he suddenly became aware
Of a woman lying close by his feet,
And he wondered who was there.

In the quiet, still darkness of midnight,
Ruth identified herself to the man,
Asked that he cover her up warmly,
Then shared a fact from Naomi's plan.

She told Boaz she knew he was kinsman,
And he picked up the thread from that point:
She had not set her eye on the rich young men,
But been kind and with Naomi remained joint.

Boaz now revealed he knew his duty,
But also that he was not nearest kin;
Ruth's reputation in the city was virtuous,
And he wanted no one to suspect any sin.

So this is what Boaz promised:
Ruth should stay through most of the night,
Then when daylight came and men moved again,
He would find the man who could settle Ruth's plight.

So Ruth lay at Boaz's feet until morning,
But arose while it was still dark:
Boaz wanted to protect her virtue,
So they whispered before even the lark.

Boaz told her to take off her apron
And hold it out as a container to fill;

He poured six measures of barley in it,
Then sent her out in the morning chill.

Ruth returned straight back to the city,
To the house with Naomi she shared;
She reported all that had happened that night,
Because it was obvious that Naomi cared.

She gave Naomi the six measures of barley,
Sent by apron from Boaz, their kin;
Naomi had Ruth sit still and relax —
This day would be a day to stay in.

Resting quietly would require much patience,
But Naomi was kind and very sure
That Boaz would settle the matter
With the nearest kin; and Ruth remained pure.

Ruth 4

Boaz went up to the city's gate,
Where all the town's business was done;
He found the next kin to Naomi,
And asked him to come sit down.

Because so much business occurred there,
The town elders gathered there, too.
Boaz had a plan of his own in mind,
For which ten of those elders would do.

He laid out the situation
For the kinsman and elders to hear:
Naomi had some land to sell
Which had belonged to her husband dear.

Boaz was giving the kinsman
First dibs on that piece of land;
The kinsman said he'd redeem it.
Then Boaz told the rest of the plan.

In buying the parcel of Naomi's land,
The purchaser got Ruth too, as wife;
For whatever reason the kinsman reneged —
He had other issues going on in his life.

It was then the custom in Israel
To confirm an agreement with a shoe;
So the kinsman bared one of his feet
To let Boaz do what he wanted to do.

The ten elders served as witnesses
To the agreement reached that day;
The kind, wise man had thought ahead
So no one could have evil to say.

He explained in detail for all to hear
What the purchase agreement entailed:
All the land of Elimelech and his two sons,
Plus Ruth, Mahlon's widow, he'd not failed.

Thus Elimelech's line would continue
Through Ruth and Boaz's seed.
Mahlon's heritage would be passed on,
And to all this the elders agreed.

They even expressed their blessings
On the plans Boaz before them laid:
They wanted Ruth to be like Leah and Rachel,
In whom Israel's twelve tribes had been made.

We know nothing about the wedding,
But we know Boaz took Ruth as his wife.
At the appropriate time God gave her a son,
And we assume in their home was no strife.

The women gathered around Naomi,
Who had become a grandma at last;
Indeed she was no longer bitter,
But blessed by the Lord so vast.

Ruth's love for Naomi had been evident
For all the town's women to see;
And they knew that this love for her mother-in-law
A source of joy would continue to be.

Naomi became the nursemaid
Of baby Obed, her infant grandson;
His name before God meant worshipper;
He was reared to know Jehovah the One.

No one had any way then of knowing
That many years way down the road,

Obed would become father to Jesse,
A man who bore a mighty load.

Jesse had in his time a family —
Eight sons of which we are told —
And the youngest of those was David,
The shepherd boy — king of old.

Thus the story of Ruth and Naomi,
With its great sadness at the outset,
Became the history of our Savior
Through David, whose throne He'll occupy yet.

About the Author

Jo Ann Sherbine has been the wife of David Sherbine for more than forty-four years. They have parented nine children: three in short-term, temporary situations; three who were adopted; and three who were home-made. Three grandchildren complete the immediate family tree.

Born and reared in Western Pennsylvania, Jo Ann and David resided for over thirty-two years in South Carolina and now live in Florida. Jo Ann received her BA in English from Eastern Baptist College (now Eastern University) and her MS in psychology from Francis Marion University. She retired from a career in public education and currently fills her time with reading, writing, knitting, counted cross-stitch, and conducting Bible studies.

Printed in the United States
By Bookmasters